The Unicorn
and the Sea

The Unicorn and the Sea

Idea by Gianfranco Ogliani
Written and illustrated by Fiona Moodie

Hutchinson

London Melbourne Auckland Johannesburg

Long, long ago, in a time when dragons roamed the earth, there lived a unicorn.

All day long he spent his time in play, galloping from the forest to the mountains, and from the mountains to the sea. But he never went too near the water because he could not swim.

Sometimes, he would just sit at the edge of the forest and watch
the other animals. Everyone seemed to have a purpose: bees
gathered nectar to make honey, goats gave milk, hens laid eggs
and sheep gave wool.

But the unicorn did nothing all day but prance and dance and frisk and play, for he was a creature of great beauty and nobody seemed to expect anything of him.

Deep in his heart the unicorn was sad and lonely and more than anything he longed to have a purpose for himself.

One dark night, the unicorn was lying down to sleep when he heard a cry: 'Help! Help!'

The unicorn stood up and raced to the edge of the forest. 'Who cries for help?' he called.

'I do,' said a small voice.

The unicorn looked up and saw a little child standing on a rock, she was shaking with cold and terror. Harpies flapped all around her: dark evil creatures, half human and half bird.

'Oh, please help me!' pleaded the child. 'The Harpies have stolen me from my father the Sea King. They are keeping me here until he agrees to give up his kingdom to them.'

The unicorn's heart went out to the child. 'Climb on to my back, little one,' he said. And before the Harpies knew what had

happened the child had leaped upon the unicorn's back and they
were away.

The unicorn was filled with pride. No one had ever asked for his
help before. At last I have a purpose, he thought.

On and on they raced through the dark forest. Chattering and screeching with anger the Harpies came after them. But they could not get near, for a unicorn with a purpose can run faster than the wind.

'Faster! Faster!' cried the foxes and the owls. 'Faster! Faster!' cried the rabbits and the squirrels. 'Faster! Faster!' cried the little child. 'There are more Harpies guarding my father. They know that he is good and kind and that he will give up his kingdom to save me.'

All night and all day the unicorn galloped without stopping. By the following evening they had reached the sea shore. Looking out across the vast water they could see the Harpies surrounding the Sea King.

'Father! Father! I'm here! I'm safe!' cried the child.

But the Sea King was too far away and too full of sorrow to hear her.

The little child looked at her friend. 'I need your help once more, Unicorn,' she said. 'It is too far for me to swim by myself; please take me to my father.'

'I can't,' replied the unicorn, full of shame. 'I am afraid of water. I cannot swim.'

The child began to cry. 'Oh, please *try*,' she begged. 'When my father sees I have returned, the kingdom will be saved and all the creatures of the sea will remain free.'

The unicorn's heart was touched. He knew that even if he managed to reach the Sea King, he would not have the strength to return to the shore. But all at once he realized that his real purpose had come at last. He must carry the child through the waves to her father. He must save the kingdom of the sea.

'Jump on my back,' he said. His big hooves hardly touched the sand and his great horn pointed towards the sky as he thundered into the waves.

The unicorn found that by galloping with all his might he could stay afloat, and soon he was swimming. It took all his strength to battle through the huge waves, but on and on he went.

'Faster! Faster!' cried the child. 'Faster! Faster!' cried the fishes in the sea. Just as the sun was setting, he came within sight of the Sea King.

The Harpies had bound the Sea King fast, but when he saw the unicorn coming through the waves his strength returned and he broke free from his ties. He held out his arms to his daughter.

'My child!' cried the Sea King, as the little girl leaped from the unicorn's back and into her father's arms. The Harpies chattered and screeched angrily. But they knew it was no use. The child had returned and their hold over the king was broken. They fled into the dark night to do evil elsewhere.

Father and child hugged each other tight. In their joy, they almost forgot the brave unicorn.

The unicorn was exhausted from his great journey. As he looked up at the moon his big eyes grew dim and his sides heaved. He felt his life was leaving him and he began to sink, down and down below the waves.

Suddenly, the child remembered her friend.

'Father, unicorns cannot breathe under water like us,' she said. 'My friend has saved me and now he is dying. We must do something.'

The Sea King stretched out his arms. 'I command that the sea greets our friend like a brother. From now on he will live with us as a creature of the sea. But should he ever wish to return to land, he will become a unicorn again. And just so everyone can recognize him both in the sea and on land, he will keep his horn.'

The unicorn closed his eyes, and when he opened them again he was no longer a unicorn, but a narwhal – a beautiful sea creature with a magnificent horn.

He chose to remain with his friends in the sea. He helped to guide lost ships back on course, and when there was a shipwreck he would rescue the sailors. His life was very happy and full of purpose.

But if one night, in the light of the moon, you happen to see a big white horse with a horn on his forehead, it could be that the unicorn has returned to land.

The narwhal really exists. It is a white whale with a long horn growing out of its upper jaw. This horn can grow up to three metres long. No one is certain what it is for.

Narwhals live in the Arctic seas, but have occasionally been seen further south. They are rather rare, because they have been hunted since the Middle Ages for their horns, which are supposed to have magic powers. Some people call the narwhal the unicorn whale.